spot

BACKYARD ANIMALS

GECKOS

by Rachel Bach

AMICUS | AMICUS INK

tail

toes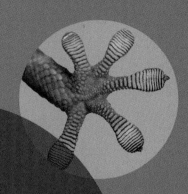

Look for these words and pictures as you read.

 eye

 skin

Have you ever seen a gecko?

A gecko is a lizard.
Geckos live in warm places.
You might see one
in Texas or Florida.

Look at the gecko's tail.
Its tail is as long as its body.

tail

skin

Look at the gecko's skin.
It is bumpy. It is soft.

Look at the gecko's toes.
They have hairy ridges.
Their feet stick to walls.

toes

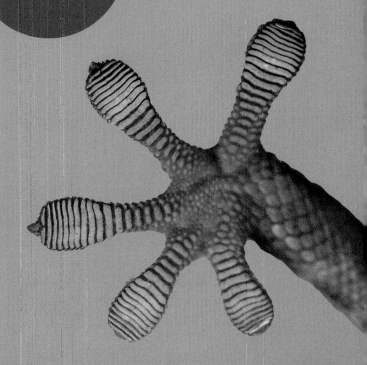

eye

Look at the gecko's eyes.
They can see in the dark.
Many geckos hunt at night.

Geckos eat bugs.
They sneak up.
Chomp!

skin

eye

Did you find?

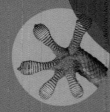

toes

tail

Spot is published by Amicus and Amicus Ink
P.O. Box 1329, Mankato, MN 56002
www.amicuspublishing.us

Library of Congress Cataloging-in-Publication Data
Names: Bach, Rachel, author.
Title: Geckos / by Rachel Bach.
Description: Mankato, Minnesota : Amicus, [2018] | Series:
   Spot. Backyard animals | Audience: Grade K-3.
Identifiers: LCCN 2016044433 (print) | LCCN 2017000792
   (ebook) | ISBN 9781681510927 (library binding) | ISBN
   9781681511825 (e-book) | ISBN 9781681522173 (pbk.)
Subjects: LCSH: Geckos--Juvenile literature.
Classification: LCC QL666.L245 B33 2018 (print) | LCC
   QL666.L245 (ebook) | DDC 597.95/2--dc23
LC record available at https://lccn.loc.gov/2016044433

Printed in the United States of America

HC   10 9 8 7 6 5 4 3 2 1
PB   10 9 8 7 6 5 4 3 2 1

Rebecca Glaser, editor
Deb Miner, series and book designer
Ciara Beitlich, production
Holly Young, production

All photos by iStock